indigo 7

indigo 7

i am

11

iUniverse, Inc.
Bloomington

indigo 7
i am

iUniverse books may be ordered through booksellers or by contacting:

iUniverse
1663 Liberty Drive
Bloomington, IN 47403
www.iuniverse.com
1-800-Authors (1-800-288-4677)

ISBN: 978-1-4620-5010-9 (sc)
ISBN: 978-1-4620-5011-6 (ebk)

Printed in the United States of America

iUniverse rev. date: 08/24/2011

2
as it is
a symphony of summary

*

listen

*

feel

*

now
come
through

6
is how
consciousness evolves
through
teaching
life
changes

activation code
take your place
fill
the
gap
contribute grace

about face

welcome back

sans back

in place

steady pace

as that
this of

both
now

accept
how

all
the
things i need
i will
receive

many things
test you know
as we learn
in due time

maintain control
absorb wisdom
use discretion
finish lesson

accept
none
envision
some

manifest an amount
greater than

controller
conductor
orchestrating
meditative
manipulation

intend
envision
thoughtform
manifestation

control

release
the

expression
of

free
being

cry
inhale yawn exhale
yawn inhale

exhale cry

release cry

repeat
cry

forget
why

yawn energize
exhale release

inhale intake
release negativity

inhale yawn
exhale cry

release
cry

clear
the
mind

sleep
awake

i am
ok

déjà vu
i wade through
all i see
until
suddenly
*

humor me
*

repeated decisions
collected mirages
*

cycles complete as processions proceed
*

look onward
savor sensation
*

watch around
smile before now
*

i have felt this before
no need to resist
*

be as do does déjà vu
*

again
*

i have done this before
*

still
i
feel
new
*

live appreciation
sense wisdom
love remembering
what is happening

disclaimer
that
is now known
*

how you change
reflects the gain
*

if
not thinking
weird is being
nothing seeing
being
as if
free
*

take what is
it is
what is
needed

energy drink
create an explosion
inside of mind
visualize intensity
absorb the find

exercise

photosynthesis

maintain the higher frequency

instrumental music helps increase

envision
self
as:
bright as light
wise as time
vibrant as sunshine
centered as sunrise
calm as sunset
live as life
ready as infinity
curious as mystery
flexible as emptiness
free-thinking as consciousness
energizing as anomalies
stimulating as time dilation
powerful as implosions
attractive as gravity
memorable as silence
imaginative as creation
rhythmic as the tide
happy inside as outside

goodness
when i sees
presently found
allowing life
in the face of
visible
knowing
the intuition being
i behold
from inside
the confines
of the
mind
I
best explanation
and
express as the
acquainted

i dreamed
an invisible being
that drew a square
in front of me

it
told me
come and see
reality

then
it motioned
the box fell back
and
slowly i
looked inside

every color
occupying all space
as each color
simultaneously changed

coming and going
subtly showing
perpetual bloom
viewing as knowing

i had a lucid dream
when
inside my palm
appeared this note
:

if this says to kill the cat
then
kill the cat
:

enter
black cat
:

proceed
attack

inside insights
inward i

want what wisdom wills within

loving living life

accepting and appreciating

remember realizations remember
your
true
nature

if you want
you can
become
without
seeing
being
as
the
one
of
nothing
living
free to
edit me
as i see
what it is
that makes we
behave
free

incarnation
be
open door
enter door
now
exit door
close door
be

i
be
in
between
opening
and
closing

kundalini serpent
present
before
being
perplexing mystery
*

curiosity
intrigued
presently
confounding
*

elusively
enlightening
paradox
*

salient
silence
stimulating
chakras
*

corpus consciousness
collective convergence
connected conscience
elevated expression
*

sense the dream
all may see
*

realize what
in the now
*

recognize how
1 is all

listen
above baseline
under top
as
i
will
allowing
of the finding
that this line
circles
nothing

none undone
source
of
the
1

once
is
then
done
by virtue of
1

all
things
1
does
come opposite
undone

as complete
cycles bind
rhythm rounds
bound
with
time

flowing matrix
thinking ocean
subtle connection
of
nothing
happening

numbers
1—recognition/no
2—yes
3—divine
4—change
5—acknowledgment (of change)
6—assistance
7—creator
8—masculine (consciousness)
9—feminine (nature)
0—unity
awareness

open this gift
the imaginary flower
the lotus
of
too many petals

pda
i do this
you do that
we do us
they do them

i am weird
you are strange

we are amazed

they are around

i am light
you are life

we are alive

they are aware

i love you
you love me
we love us
as
they
can
see

presentation
communication
entrainment
language

representation
wardrobe
hygiene
diet

exercise

rest

repeat

reap

consciousness
conveyed
consciously
raised

prisms
illuminate
being

3 sided 5

illuminate
spectral
life

reflective vision
made of reason
changing seasons
place of being

this is
still playing
without saying
what the reason
is
for being
as reflections
of
the

request
the perfect haircut
everyone hears nothing
watch as they
depart from the matter
content with whatever

righteous 1's
recognize religions
as perspectives of
that which is
beyond right and wrong

self-discovery
show me
synergy
4
i allow privilege
to be
me
4
i accept all
as
3
forgotten memories
cast shade
over
4
always
2
lead the way
to
what
is
5

set fire to desire
place the ground around the hole
take the flow out of control
I
am
the illusory mask of 0 folds
placed upon
1
before
day
1

I am again

i am the game

1
in
the
same

spar
match frequency
increase accordingly

when in sync
both admit success
repeat
rest
repeat
grace now moves with speed

if momentarily lost
1 accepts defeat
rest
repeat
rest
strength is also weakness

-life is a dream
~i am lucid

-i understand
~i know nothing

-this is me
~i do think

-you are free
~yes indeed

-i digress
~i do see

sustain physical
continue embracing
work focusing
time providing
task completion
upon releasing
concern free
work
is
complete

sustain mental
maintain intention
mind focusing
thought unending
attraction happening
upon continuing
being free
thought
is
manifesting

thank you
no thank you

the big bang
prime
procession
as
the
1
sided
1
expounds
self
now

the dreamscape
is
a
subjective school

the lifetime
is
a
class in session

1

accepts

or

will
repeat

as

lessons
intensify

until i realize

think
i left yesterday.
i am of today.
i am behind tomorrow.
where do i stay?

trees
breathe
being

showing
working
reality

grounded
being
making
ceiling

seeds embody insight
water and light ignite
life

unveiled
i
is
I
not

I
now
mind
time

i
not
exist
veiled

vision cleared
fear transmuted

i am weird
never scared

take my dare
face your fear

show the world
you are here

wants need seeds
everything i need
presents itself
before
me

greetings
want

meet my
thought

i let it become
as i think

i continue intending
until
it is
upon
me

then

i smile as i remember
nurturing a seed
being
easy

when i write
i
am
neither
here
nor
there

i feel my mind
verb paired adjective

i feel as if
i hear
no sound

i
attain
insight
accessible
inside
i

writer's block
free mind feels
rest time works
feel time work
rest free mind

still time thinks
free mind hears
mind stills time
free hear thoughts

sit
crawl
walk
run
fly
thrive
sit
still

writing intuition
tantalizing
tranquility
hypnotizes
me
as
something
somewhere
simulates
situations
i
can
translate
as clear
as
i
see
so
you can
resonate
with
the
harmony

XI
abstract reality
mirage mentality
think lightning without sound
observational
silent sounding how
inquisitive
i am
dreaming thinking
metaphorical thing
i am weird
this is true
*

so

are

you

yoga
graceful
posing
causing
focusing

inside
outward

sustain
breathwork

sweating
stretching

i am
smiling

i am
master
of this
body

it is
something
how much
i love
breathing
in sync

you are welcome
as
you
are

i am
is i
if i
accept

we are
as we
if we
will be

if you
see me
we can
be we
somewhere
between
observing
and
caring

you see my body
the riddle of scars
you see my imperfection
as
lesson remnants
change my skin
as the memories
stay with me
i
allow
the
understanding
of my journey
changing shape
stay with me
changing ways
patience
is
what
i
became

philosophy

-basically-
remember here
come here
now stays here
what happens here

-being-
we are part of this
regardless of acceptance
to accept is to be
resistance is being partially

-chess-
i play
as a pawn
until i remember
to transform

-conspiracy theory-
continue revealing
as the awakening
will verify
finding

-half full-
make the
half that is lacked
with the
half that is had

-motivational-
i must
act now
as time is
of the essence

-music-
all is expression
existence is vibration
resonance is harmony
rhythm is everything
remain in sync

-onion-
i form an onion
light is my center
layers consist of wisdom
i attain focus inward

-procrastination-
i
have
time

-yoga-
balance exertion
now
enjoy benefit
later

ZEN STANCE
stop when i start
start when i stop

allow the new standard

weird and normal remain subjective

ordinary always changes

travel lightly
change
being

understanding may induce smiling

*

yawning can signify recognition

**

sleeping helps

*   *   *

change comes

*   *   *

it is what it is

the playful penname
plays through writing
as others reading
what they are
finding
**

depending on
state of mind
parallels plausible
subject
of and to
change
*

everyone hears
many are told
wise 1's accept
regardless

experience the subtlety
of what is
happening
through the complexity
of what is
becoming

balance	listen
self	intuition
integrate	quiet
spiritual	ego
physical	relinquish
mental	control
meditate	accept
unique	knowledge
become	beyond
awakened	knowing

i appear as i am
i am not as i will be

i think i am me
i know i am thought

allow
as it is
accepting

mental state
integrate
meditative grace

health affects presence
diet affects energy
mind changes everything

behavior
now
determines
how
1
will change
when time comes
age

fear of death
i am not saying i am afraid
i am not saying i am not afraid
funny death

why
not
be concerned
*

consider every possibility
*

why not
some
might be right

infinity
symbolized
is seen as
2
circles
tucked
in
side
1

being of interconnectivity
accept
that
only
this
can
be

in the room you are in
everything fades away
accept the sound
you are that loud

intuition
synchronicity

i know naught of what i do
this makes me laugh
how
are
you
?

prana of maya
breath of life
light the fire
from
on
1
3
5
higher

i know why
i like storms
how
explains
why
i feel storms

as
the
one
being

i
am
always
free

i find existing encouraging

the allure of life
the feeling surrounding
what is inside
countenance

i am here
this i see
all naught is
everything

if this book would end
i could stop waiting to finish

never fear

humility humbles dignity

respectfully

open mouth
no sound

look around
life lives

ponder words
certain clear

remove there
reside here

totally
takes
this
place

recognize paths
bow to grace

change ~ consciousness ~ infinite
sound ~ vibration ~ resonance
love ~ light ~ life

some stay where they were
others move where they are

i cannot appreciate yes
until i understand no

desire nothing
appreciate everything

when in doubt
remember
karma

experiencing is understanding
being is knowing
remembering is explaining
living is changing
allowing is learning
becoming is existing
existence is experience
experience is to be understood

feel the love

always is when
now is how
mind is where
this is what
all is
who
you are

sharing thoughts remains fulfilling
as
does
laughing

you bow
i
bow

you yawn
i
yawn

quiet mind knowing
tell me something
i know nothing

so still
change
sounds
near

1111

3
autonomous prime
recollected rhyme
come inside
then perceive
that i write
three sounds more
circling
thinking
assisting
being

2

running down the street i find
grapefruits at my feet continue
down the street before my
endurance captures me

chill

as the wise 1's say
have a weird day
resume the array
forget what i say
do this
everyday

1
every tree is different

fingernails are helpful

as the fear of mastery goes
i accept

now i

i do

i flow

now i

i
go

how important is this timing
realigning
i write what i hear
quiet whispering ear

i once heard a wise 1 say
chill out dog you got the bone
it made no sense
until i laughed alone

desire escape search
escape search desire
search desire escape

soon it will happen
resist nothing resisting
so
distort the change accordingly
or
embrace the choice

change paths to play the game
changing paths will change your game
end the games
by
realizing the change

a walking bird approaches to see
fruit falling from a tree hit me
expressing the being the
tree

how much more is what i write
complicate the situation
with what i do not
hide

come this way
we
form
prophecy

artificial lighting hiding darkness
sedentary lifestyle plan
winter hibernation den
wake with outdoor lighting

you made the chance you had to win
output reflects intake
attain
now reveals all
ways
that the empty
is remaining
as the answers
that are changing
as your mystery
is unfolding
as your own life story

when we meet
i invite you
accept or decline
i will be seeing you in time

the writings of my invisible arm
well
no pressure to start off with
as
i move simultaneously
so
your arm is the 1 writing
the
evidence you think you are finding

the watchful i
hello
i respect you for seeing me
as
i know where you go to hide
from
everyone
seeing you act new
as opposed to
looking through
eyes
to speak to
you who knows
i
am
too

the tip of the present
before
shadows
appear

the fight from the dog
what the fuck are you looking at
?
you think you see me
!
i see you
naked
!!
mind still shaken
mystery
awaken
. . .
come on then
.
step forward
.
follow that noise that comes too close
.
make me show you me on you
.
bark
what now
! !
growl
yeah i see you
! !
sneeze
when i get loose

rorrimirror
of the all
what is this
after all

of this life
embrace
silence

all the of
this is what
all after

paper thought
i twirl my fine point pen along my fingers from end to end
i see the potential of the paper sustained
then
i relate
what it will be
as i express the
creativity.
yes?
which is mightier
the pen or the paper?
probably the writer
i prefer paper
for being accepting
as the former imposes
lasting expressions of latent ideas
set
between the lines
of the rhymes
saved on paper
true
you
hear these words
but
how
do they reach you
?

lost condition
it was here
receding something left me searching
think
i am
it was
something
i will find it
come on
think!
i once thought i had forgot
think
clocks are ticking
stop the waiting
all are breathing
get in sync.
ok
accept.
ok
empty.
nothing
indeed.

look
into
my
eyes
as
i
do
this

watch
my eyes
scan your thoughts

watch my eyes
scan your body

slowly

watch my eyes
watching yours
as you
watch me smile
with my being
to
enjoy
the
charge i gave you

it's ok
laugh if you care
go ahead
i am still here

i do
see
that you
see
inside the mind of light shining time
seeing
as i
see
that with which i change i by
sees
science
seeing
being
see
through

hippy hug love
envelope the earth in your energy
absorb the hurt you cause your earth
you cut the trees you cherish as wares
you burn the toxins polluting your air
but know this
you can change this
if you
think
this

have you done
what now fun
all enjoy
seeing
1
writing
insightful rhyming
reaching worldwide
assisting any mind
aware
of
the light
inside

feisty fire
vibing
flirting
desire
building
oh
to hold it
what is given
oh
keep going
senses presenting
ah
no stop now
i am waiting
ha
alright then
again

expressive ink
receptive paper
complex short hand
fine point pen
spiral notepad
empty my mind
now begins
as i write
line!
where was i?
i drift in and out.

excusing a secret
if i
told you
i had to
could it suffice
to say
please
do not look
that way
?

did you think this?
welcome to your mind
what?
i gave you my thought
how?
i saw an opening
how?
by not saying
what?
words
like?
now
and?
here
not fair
think less
how so?
like
this

breathe breath
you are
breath
that you
breathe
change the seed you will repeat
breath
i am
breath
change me see such that i reach
breathe
relief
breath
that you
breathe
as i
breathe
of our
breath
of
progress

alpha
i
am
my superior
the arbiter of
my disposition
doubt
me
not
once less
become more
assess the best
allow the rest
observing self
as is always
remain lucid
with respect to
choosing your battles
never fight time
humble yourself
the rest will come
change every opportunity
assist peers with subtle guidance
allow opinions to guard your presence
be a happily silent expression
the 1 thought proper
i
embody
power

a public service announcement
the upside down nametag stating
change is coming
as is what is becoming

remember

cherish love

give
of
self

show
living inspired by truth
true
glimpses into
you
becoming aware
as the change
so
strive for balance or be lopsided

a letter to you know who
i do know
that
this
finds
you

i wish i did not know
that
you are allowed to be

profit versus life
we know which will die

what is
will be
until we
change

see

as i love you
i
allow
you

so

go

now

before you disappear

2

pause for the cause punctuated by cheers and applause
unable to return where once hid then
time wise mind residing present tense
savor the presence of history's lessons
the intriguingly subtle mystery being

1
attention reviewing nothing
it is subtle and you enjoy it
feel free to see me think you see this
already happened before you thought it

expand perspective
enhance the collective

2
complete

1
things thought
between worlds
:

until next time

~11~